Love + blessings [signature] 6/14/2022

Witness the Most Powerful YOU

Five Fundamental Principles to Create and Live the Life You Desire

Eva M. Kennedy

Witness the Most Powerful You
Five Fundamental Principles to Create and Live the Life You Desire

Eva M. Kennedy

Copyright © 2016 Eva M. Kennedy

All rights reserved. No part of this book may be used or reproduced in any manner without the written permission of the author, except in the case of quotations.

Published by:
1Evalution Publishing,
a subsidiary of Eva M. Kennedy LLC,
Chicago, Illinois
www.1Evalution.com

Printed in the United States of America

Cover design and layout by: TheBookProducer.com

ISBN: 0-692-78884-0
ISBN 13: 978-0-692-78884-4

Library of Congress Control Number: 2016918455

∼

*When you let go of the fear and take action to move forward, you will realize the universe has been waiting to welcome you home.
The universe feeds the soul.*
~ Eva M. Kennedy

CONTENTS

Introduction 7

Five Fundamental Principles 8-10

Awareness 11-22

Clarity 23-36

Alignment 37-42

Authenticity 43-54

Enlightenment 55-62

Summary 63-66

Bibliography 67

About the Author 69

INTRODUCTION

If you want to make meaningful changes and live the life you desire, *Witness the Most Powerful You* helps you take the next steps.

Each day you choose how to live your life based on the decisions you make. You decide whether you want more out of life or to maintain the status quo. *Witness the Most Powerful You* is an ongoing self-development process based on five fundamental principles. These principles are designed to help you make decisions and choices by focusing on the person within.

Witness the Most Powerful You creates awareness and provides the tools and structure to complete assessments and develop action plans to make positive changes. The program will help you make the right decisions and choices to achieve your personal and professional goals. The five principles build off one another. You will go through a series of eye-opening activities and answer thought-provoking questions. These activities promote powerful self-discovery to focus on the person within. You will see if your life is out of balance, define your top five values, and make decisions and commitments to improve your brand. Your vision, goals, and purpose will be defined. Most significantly, you will understand why it is so important to be your authentic self. Know that you have everything within to achieve what you desire.

Going through this process is rewarding but can be emotional and challenging, especially if you are stepping outside your comfort zone. Keep in mind that it can also be stressful and unfulfilling when you want to make changes in your life but continue to maintain the status quo.

Life is an ongoing process of evolution. *Witness the Most Powerful You* will help you to grow and create the life you desire.

FIVE FUNDAMENTAL PRINCIPLES

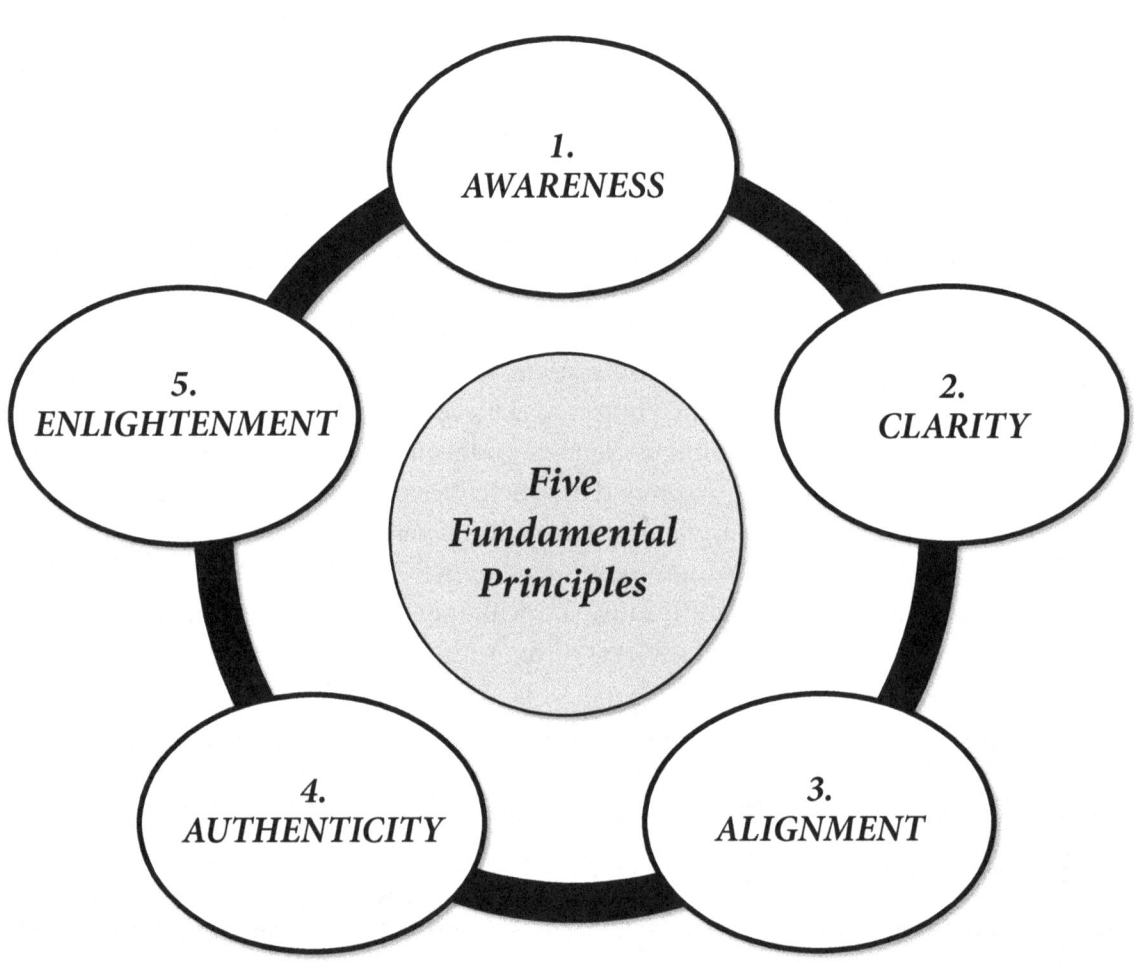

FIVE FUNDAMENTAL PRINCIPLES
Approach: Create and live the life you desire.

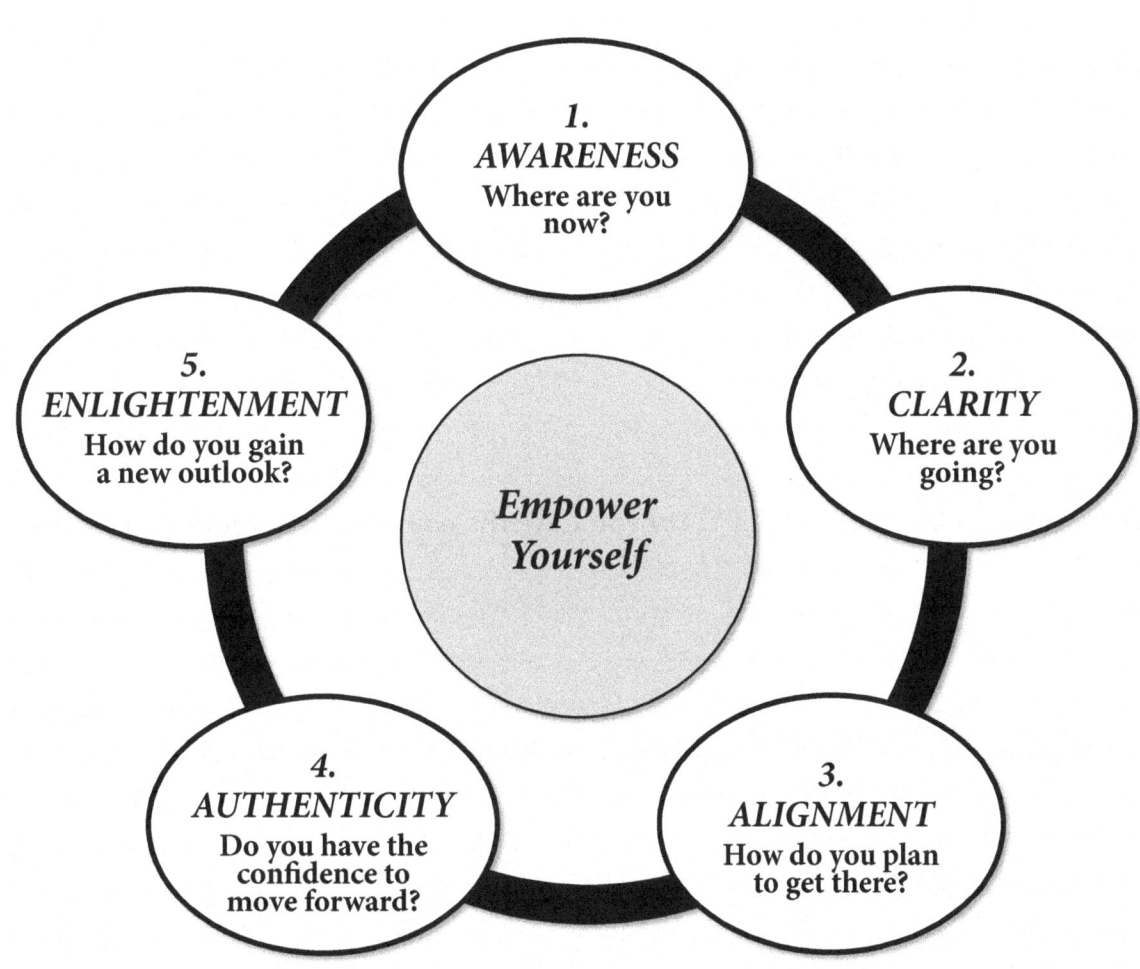

Five Fundamental Principles

FIVE FUNDAMENTAL PRINCIPLES
Outline:

Principle 1. **AWARENESS: Where are you now?**
- Balance
- Values
- Brand

Principle 2. **CLARITY: Where are you going?**
- Vision
- Goals
- Purpose

Principle 3. **ALIGNMENT: How do you plan to get there?**
- Reexamine
- Connect
- Confirm

Principle 4. **AUTHENTICITY: Do you have the confidence to move forward?**
- Acknowledge
- Surrender
- Embrace

Principle 5. **ENLIGHTENMENT: How do you gain a new outlook?**
- Live in the moment
- Harmony
- Gratitude

Principle 1.
AWARENESS

Where are you now?

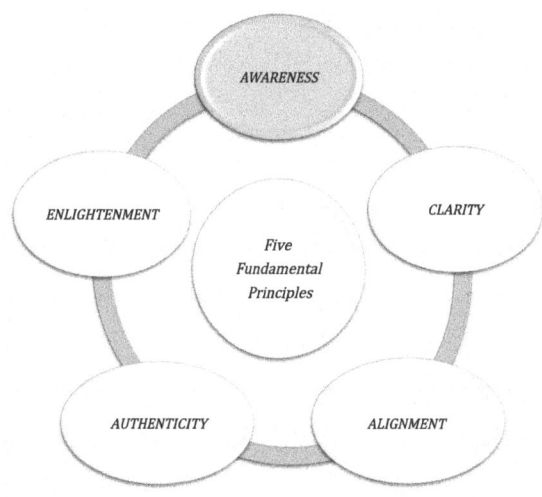

Working to achieve greater balance in life, making decisions that are aligned with your values, and improving your brand are starting points in working toward what you want to achieve.

To understand this principle, you will be given the tools to help you assess and define certain aspects of your life, such as what is important to you, your principles, and how you see yourself. This exercise will assist you in making important decisions going forward.

You will assess where your life may be out of balance and learn how to create more stability. You will define your top five values, which will help you make meaningful decisions and commitments. Your brand provides the opportunity for you to see how you show up to others so that what people see in you is what you want them to see

Awareness focuses on balance, values, and brand.

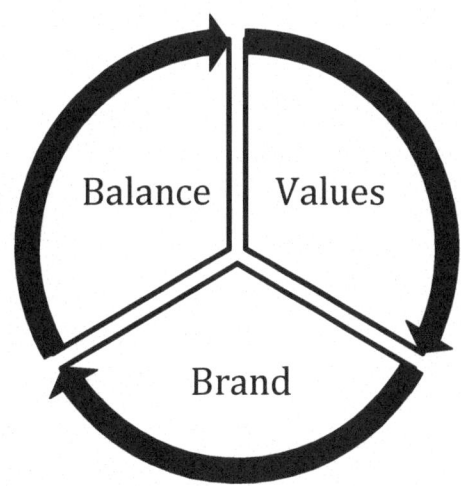

AWARENESS

Purpose:

Balance – Helps you focus on where and how to spend your time based on what's important to you.

Values – Identify, prioritize, and improve the most important areas of your life.

Brand – Provides the opportunity to evaluate self.

Actions:

Balance – Identify where your life may be out of balance, and decide what aspects need more or less focus.

Values – Define your top ten values, and prioritize the top five.

Brand – Define the characteristics, and identify how to improve your personal brand.

Intended outcomes:

Balance – Have more balance in your life.

Values – Make consistent decisions, and take committed actions aligned with your values.

Brand – Understand the real power of *you*.

AWARENESS
Balance:

Balance allows you to focus and plan in the areas that are most important to you. Balance should be assessed over a period of time. Concentrate on patterns of behavior that will help you learn more about yourself and how to spend your time to live a more balanced life. Keep in mind that life is fluid, circumstances may change, and trying to live a balanced life can be an ongoing challenge.

Wheel of life: A tool for helping you examine areas of your life that may be out of balance.

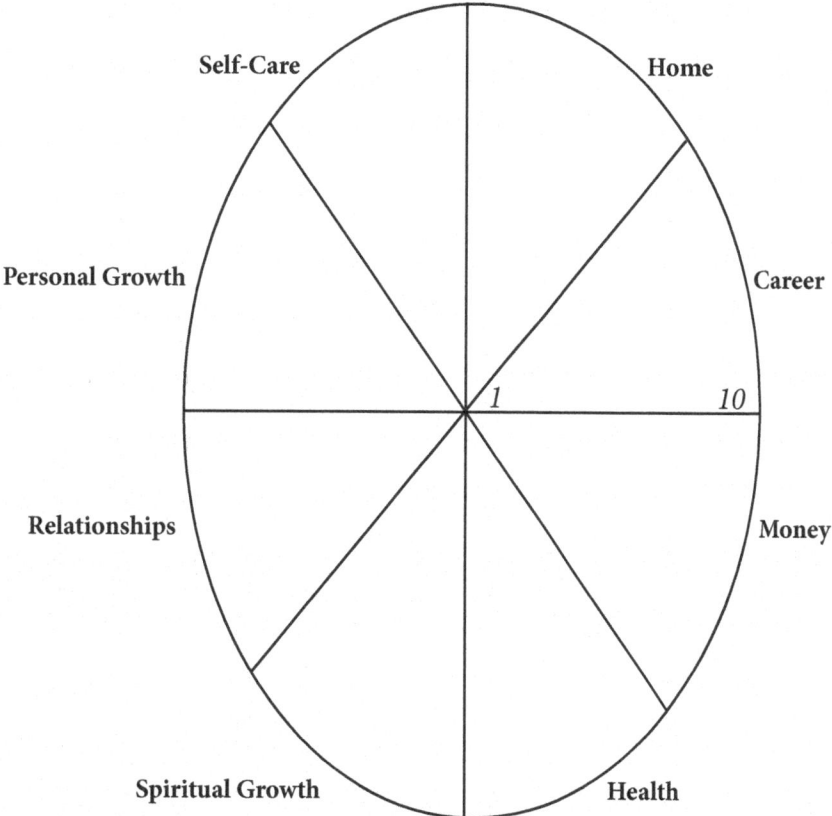

Directions: Review the eight sections of the wheel. The sections represent different aspects of your life. Seeing the center of the wheel as one (the lowest) and the outer edges as ten (the highest), rank your level of satisfaction. Mark each section with an *X* indicating your level of satisfaction. Once you have completed ranking all sections, draw a line around the circle connecting to each *X*. The new perimeter represents the wheel of your life. (Feel free to add or remove any areas from the wheel. This wheel should represent areas that are most important to you.)

AWARENESS
Balance:

1. As you look at the wheel, what do you notice about the shape of the wheel that the numbered rankings made? What stands out in your wheel's balance?

   _____
   _____
   _____

2. What would have to happen for you to experience more balance in each of these areas in your life? Is there a particular area(s) you will focus on?

   _____
   _____
   _____

3. How will you balance competing demands?

   _____
   _____
   _____

4. What help and support from others will you need, if any?

   _____
   _____
   _____

5. What patterns of behavior have you identified and will have to address to have more balance in that area(s)? What actions will you take?

   _____
   _____
   _____

6. What commitment will you make to having a more balanced life? How flexible are you? When will you take action?

   _____
   _____
   _____

❖ When you are prompted to make decisions, you may ask yourself the following questions: Will the outcome bring greater balance in my life? Will the outcome bring less balance in my life?

AWARENESS
Values:

Your values represent who you are; they are your core beliefs. *Success on and off the job requires knowing and understanding your values.* They provide some standard for determining what is right for you. It is important to know what personal values you are committed to, both on and off the job. Values allow you to make decisions and prioritize what is important in the way you live and work. They provide clarity and focus. It is important to make life decisions that are aligned with who you are, which is essential to creating and living the life you desire. Making decisions that go against your values may cause discomfort and unhappiness. As you grow and gain a deeper understanding of self, your values may change.

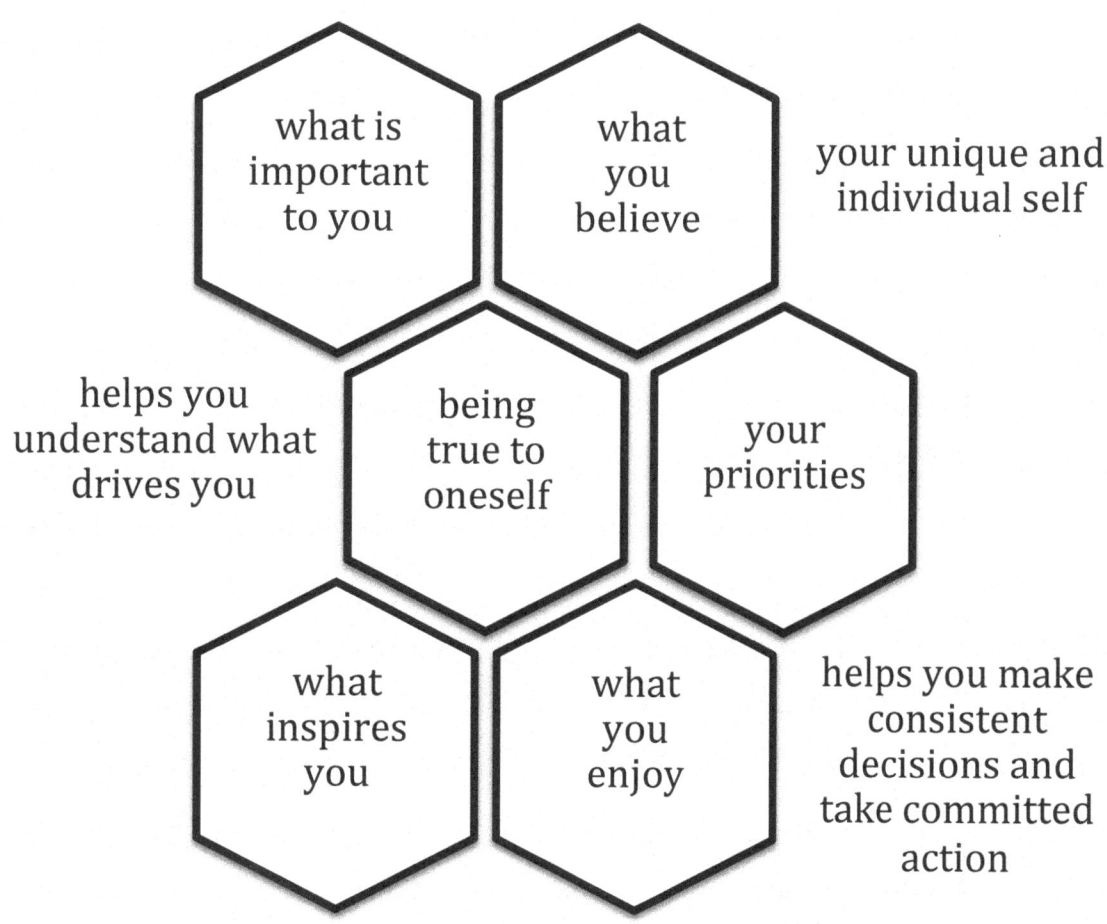

Principle 1. AWARENESS

AWARENESS
Values:

Define your values.

Step 1.
Use the list below to select the ten values that you most identify with. Add to the list if one of your top values is not included.

Academics	Job security
Achievement	Joy
Acknowledgment	Knowledge
Affection	Leadership
Appreciation	Loyalty
Challenges	Meaningful work
Community	Morals
Compassion	Personal development
Competition	Physical challenge
Cooperation	Pleasure
Creativity	Power and authority
Democracy	Privacy
Dignity	Public service
Effectiveness	Quality relationships
Ethical standards	Recognition
Excellence	Religion
Excitement	Reputation
Faith	Responsibility
Family	Security
Financial freedom	Self-respect
Friendships	Serenity
Growth	Spirituality
Health	Stability
Helping others	Status
Honesty	Support
Independence	Time
Influencing others	Truth
Inner harmony	Wealth
Integrity	Wisdom
Intellectual	Working with others

AWARENESS
Values:

Step 2.

Prioritize your top five values.
Now that you have identified ten values, can you narrow the list to your top five?

To help you identify your top five values, consider the following:

1. Review the list of your top ten values and think about what is really important to you.

2. Think about times when you were happy, proud, fulfilled, and satisfied, and you felt powerful.
   - What were you doing?
   - Why were these moments important to you?
   - Were there other people sharing these moments?
   - Who were they?
   - Why were these people important to you?
   - What factors contributed to these feelings of happiness, pride, and the like?

3. Based on your answer to the previous question, circle the five values that represent what is most important to you. If you could only satisfy one of these values, which one would it be? This answer is your first value; continue the process until you have listed five values in order of priority.

Prioritize, list, and define your top five values. Start by listing the most important first and continue until you have selected the top five. (For example, "Family—to spend time with my family.")

1. _____

2. _____

3. _____

4. _____

5. _____

AWARENESS
Values:

1. What are your observations about how your values represent what is most important to you in the way you live and work?

   _____
   _____
   _____

2. What values are you not honoring, and what is the impact of this in the way you live and work?

   _____
   _____
   _____

3. How do your values show up through what is expected of you in the workplace and in your relationships with others?

   _____
   _____
   _____

4. How will you use your values to make decisions going forward? How will they make a difference in the way you live and work?

   _____
   _____
   _____

5. How does the act of defining and prioritizing your values help you move in the direction of creating your best life?

   _____
   _____
   _____

6. What have you learned from this experience?

   _____
   _____
   _____

   ❖ **When you are prompted to make decisions, you may ask yourself the following questions: Is this decision aligned with my values? Does this decision go against my values?**

AWARENESS
Brand:
The Power of *You*

Brand is how people evaluate and view one another. You must be clear about the image you want to project and be consistent across all interactions and profiles, especially given the impact of social media. You can manage your personal brand. It is important for you to be aware of how you show up to others.

Tom Peters states it clearly: "You are the owner and responsible for the brand *you*." Regardless of age or where you are in life, whether you are in the workplace or not, everyone needs to understand the importance of branding.

Living your brand directs you to live authentically in all aspects of your life. Your brand can help you build confidence and use your innate strengths to increase your visibility. Your brand is held in the minds of those who know you. You need to be aware of their perceptions to understand your brand.

As you focus on the life you desire, think about your brand and how you can improve it.

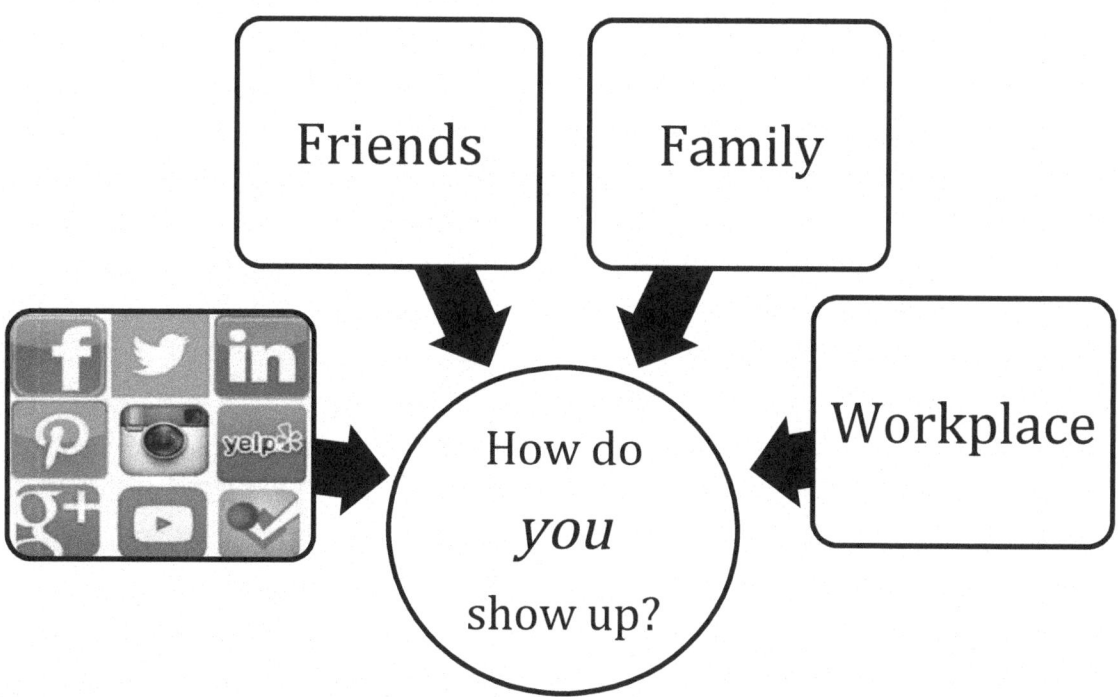

AWARENESS

Brand:

Starting today, think of yourself as having a brand. The more you are aware of your values and brand, the more responsible you are to hold yourself accountable for your decisions, actions, and performance, both at home and in the workplace. When thinking of your brand, consider these factors: Are you a good person? Do you do your best work? Do you deliver value to the customer? Are you developing your skills? How are you distinguishing yourself from others?

This exercise can be used to help strengthen your brand in both personal and professional relationships. If you are truly interested in improving your brand, get feedback from your manager, peers, employees, family, and friends. Have an open discussion about how they view you as compared to how you view yourself. This exchange can be used as an opportunity for you to improve and grow your brand and to discuss perceptions, generational differences, and expectations. However, you must be open and receptive to the comments. Just as a company solicits feedback from customers to improve its products and services, you solicit feedback to improve your personal brand.

1. When you think of your favorite brand (such as BMW, Samsung, Apple), what are the characteristics of the brand you identify with and ultimately purchase? Why did you select that brand?

   _____
   _____
   _____

2. Think of yourself as your favorite brand. What are some of the qualities of the *you* brand?

   _____   _____
   _____   _____
   _____   _____

3. How do others perceive and describe the *you* brand in the workplace? (Solicit feedback from at least five individuals in the workplace, such as your peers, managers, or employees.)

   _____   _____
   _____   _____
   _____   _____

AWARENESS
Brand:

4. How will you integrate this feedback into your brand to be your best in the workplace? Be specific.

    What area(s) will you focus on? What actions will you take? By when?

    _____   _____
    _____   _____
    _____   _____

5. How do family and friends perceive and describe the you brand? (Solicit feedback from five family members and friends.)

    _____   _____
    _____   _____
    _____   _____

6. How will you integrate this feedback into your brand to be your best with family and friends? Be specific.

    What area(s) will you focus on? What actions will you take? By when?

    _____   _____
    _____   _____
    _____   _____

7. What is the *you* brand? How does the *you* brand show up across all interactions? (Write a statement that best describes your brand—a tagline.)

    _____
    _____
    _____

8. What commitments will you make to grow the *you* brand? How important is this to you? Why?

    _____
    _____
    _____

❖ When you are prompted to make decisions, you may ask yourself the following questions: Will this decision improve my brand? Will this decision hurt my brand?

NOTES:

Principle 2.
CLARITY

Where are you going?

When you are clear about what you want and if you are committed and disciplined, you will get positive results. By knowing what you want to achieve, you will know where to concentrate your efforts and will recognize distractions.

When exploring this principle, you will be provided with the tools to help you focus on what you want and where you want to go. Discovering your purpose is a natural evolution in your journey to living a better life.

To move forward, first you will define your vision or what you want out of life. Next you will identify your top three goals. Setting goals is a powerful process to plan your future and turn your vision into reality. Finally, as you continue to improve your life, you may want to explore your purpose, the reason you exist.

Clarity focuses on your vision, goals, and purpose.

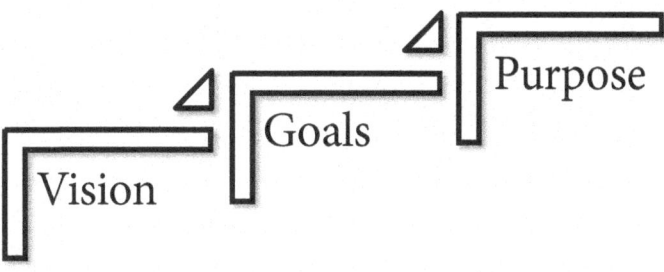

CLARITY
Purpose:

Vision – Helps you define what you truly desire.

Goals – Allow you to plan to achieve what you desire.

Purpose – Helps you focus and move forward in a positive way.

Actions:

Vision – Capture the vision you already have within you.

Goals – Set three goals to help you stay focused and concentrate your efforts on what is important.

Purpose – Define your purpose.

Intended outcomes:

Vision – Know the vision you have for your life.

Goals – Have a plan for the future; know where to concentrate your efforts, and measure achievements along the way.

Purpose – Live more authentically with a greater sense of meaning.

CLARITY
Vision: What is it that you really want to achieve?

Defining your vision may not come easily. If you are one of those individuals who has a difficult time defining your vision, know that you are not alone. You may not have the confidence that you can achieve your vision, or you just don't know what steps to take to make meaningful life changes. You may also have doubt and fear of failure and rejection, or you may think you are not worthy of the desires of your heart. As a result, you are unable to move forward. However, deep down inside, you know you have more to offer and want more out of life. You haven't given up and are looking for help.

This is so important: **Believe.** You are deserving. You are worthy. You can achieve whatever is in your heart. If you are passionate and committed about your dream, you can achieve it.

Step 1.

Vision exercise: This will help you connect to the desire you already have in your heart. Sit quietly, close your eyes and inhale and exhale softly. As you listen to the sound of your breathing, clear your mind and begin to imagine your life 40 years from now. Imagine your life unfolded just how you wanted it to. As you sit and look back over your life, you smile, pleased with how your life unfolded, think of the following;

- What made you smile?
- What have you accomplished?
- What did you do that made you feel good about your life?
- What type of person are you?
- How did you live your life?
- What matters most to you?
- What value did you add to others?
- What's the wisdom and guidance for you?

When you are ready, write down all the details. The more details you can write down, the more fulfilling and inspiring the vision will be.

What is your vision?

_____
_____
_____

CLARITY

Vision: What is it that you really want to achieve?

Step 2.

- Repeat step 1. Do not think about *doubt, fear,* or *"I can't." Think about what is possible.* Allow all of you to be present, focus on having a clear vision, and include any additional details.
- Don't allow your present situation to dictate what you want to achieve in the future.
- Acknowledge, name, and embrace the emotions and feelings that emerge. (Emotions will be discussed further in Principle 4, Authenticity.)
  - Meditate daily on your vision, and become comfortable with it.
  - Use a vision board, and place it where you can see it night and day.
  - Read your vision out loud daily.
  - Accept and own your vision.

Include additional details of your vision:

_____
_____
_____
_____
_____
_____
_____
_____

CLARITY
Vision: What is it that you really want to achieve?

1. How important is it for you to achieve your vision? How committed are you to making your vision a reality?

   _____
   _____
   _____

2. In the way you live and work, what is the biggest obstacle preventing you from achieving your vision? What action(s) will you take?

   _____
   _____
   _____

3. What is the impact of not achieving your vision?

   _____
   _____
   _____

4. What do you need to achieve your vision but don't have yet? (For example, resources, finances, training, skills experience, certifications, opportunity)

   _____
   _____
   _____

5. What do you have but don't need? (For example, time, stress, lack of confidence, or anything that may be getting in the way)

   _____
   _____
   _____

❖ Defining your vision provides a clear picture of what you truly want. This vision will help you make decisions going forward. When you are prompted to make decisions, you may ask yourself the following questions: Is this decision aligned with my vision? Is this decision contrary to my vision?

CLARITY
Goals: Plan for your future.

1. What has to happen within the next year for you to feel like you are making progress in achieving your goals?

   _____
   _____
   _____

2. Establish goals that will achieve the vision you hold in your heart. They can provide motivation and increase self-confidence. Goals are actions and experiences that provide ongoing progress to keep you on target to achieve your vision.

   Considering the following for goal setting:

   - Establish three goals.
   - Focus on annual goals.
   - Review and evaluate goals every nine months to prepare for annual goal setting.
   - Establish new annual goals, if applicable, each year.

   SMART is a powerful approach to setting goals.

   S – Specific: What do you want to achieve? Why is this goal important to you?
   M – Measurable: How will you measure your goal? How will you know when you have achieved it?
   A – Attainable: How will you attain this goal? What actions will you take?
   R – Relevant: Is this goal achievable and aligned with what is important to you? How?
   T – Time bound: When will this goal be accomplished? What is your deadline?

CLARITY
Goals: Plan for your future.

List three goals to be achieved within the next twelve months.
What will you commit to?

Within the next twelve months, what achievements or events would support bringing your vision closer to reality? Be specific.	Is this goal achievable and aligned with what is important to you? How?	When will this goal be accomplished? What is your deadline?	How will you measure your goal? How will you know when you have achieved it?
1.			
2.			
3.			

CLARITY
Goals: Plan for your future.

1. What can you start doing that will help you achieve your goals?

   _____
   _____
   _____

2. What can you stop doing that will help you achieve your goals?

   _____
   _____
   _____

3. What can you continue to do that will help you achieve your goals?

   _____
   _____
   _____

4. What can sabotage your achievement of these goals? What patterns of behavior, obstacles, challenges, or resources might get in the way? How will you handle it? What actions will you take?

   _____
   _____
   _____

5. What is the best advice or motivation you can say to yourself that will help you achieve these goals? (For example, "Stay the course," "I can do it," "Take one day at a time," or "Keep going.")

   _____
   _____
   _____

Note: Read your goals every morning. It will help you stay focused and move in the direction of what is visible to you that day for achieving your goals.

CLARITY
Goals: Plan for your future.

1. Think about what help you may need to get started. What ongoing support and encouragement will you need? Who will you reach out to? (For example, an accountability partner, coach, peer, family, friends, therapist, mentor)

   Who: _____ Specific support: _____

   Who: _____ Specific support: _____

   Who: _____ Specific support: _____

2. What resources do you already have to help you achieve your goals?

   _____
   _____
   _____

3. What strengths will need to be maximized to be effective and achieve your goals? How will you be able to maximize these strengths? (For example, training, formal education, or more practice)

   _____
   _____
   _____

CLARITY
Goals: Plan for your future.

1. As you think about how you will attain your top three goals, think of small steps you can take to help you get started. What actions can you commit to and achieve within the next 30 days?

   Action 1: _____ by when: _____

   Action 2: _____ by when: _____

   Action 3: _____ by when: _____

2. How likely are you to achieve your goals? Rate your likelihood of achievement on a scale of one to five. If rating is below a four, carefully examine the barriers and refocus.

   _____
   _____
   _____

3. What are the consequences of not achieving your goals? How will you handle not reaching a goal?

   _____
   _____
   _____

4. What will you do to celebrate and acknowledge yourself for achieving even the smallest milestone?

   _____
   _____
   _____

❖ **Setting goals gives you an approach to achieve your vision. When you are prompted to make decisions, you may ask yourself the following questions: Is this decision aligned with my goals? Is this decision going to hinder achieving my goals?**

CLARITY
Purpose: Discover your purpose.

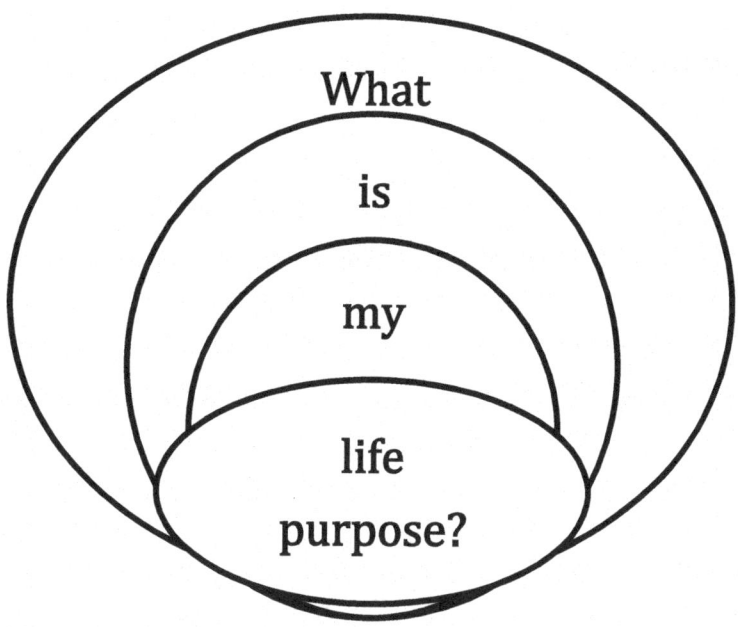

Why do I want to discover my purpose in life?

These are questions you may ask yourself as you try to live more authentically, with a greater sense of purpose and fulfillment. Discovering your purpose increases awareness of living.

Discovering your purpose is not easy, and it can take time. One approach to discovering your purpose is to connect to your authentic self; think about what you are passionate about and what talents you possess that will allow you to live the fullest expression of self. This can be done through daily meditation, which will help keep you focused and moving forward in a positive way.

CLARITY

Purpose: Discover your purpose.

The common-thread approach will give you some context about discovering your life purpose.

Careful thoughts:
- Keep your mind in an open place.
- Let your creativity flow.
- Listen to your inner voice.
- Take a hard look at your answers below.
- Pull out common thoughts and threads.
- When you find your purpose, it will resonate deeply.

1. What are you passionate about?

2. If you could do anything in the world, describe the one thing you long to do?

3. What would you do if you knew, without any doubts, that you would be successful?

4. What activities set your soul on fire?

5. What are you doing when you completely lose track of time because you are immersed in a state of creativity and joy?

CLARITY
Purpose: Discover your purpose.

6. What did you love deep down before societal pressures made you get practical?

   _____
   _____
   _____

7. Review and take a hard look at all your answers, and reflect on your words, expressions, emotions, and common threads.

   - What gifts do you possess?
   - What do you want to do with these gifts?
   - Who do you want to help?
   - What value will you add?

   My life purpose:

   Write a purpose statement below, and repeat it until you feel it in your core. Your purpose may not come to you right away, but continue to focus on your passion and what drives you. Eventually you will know your purpose. It will resonate with you deeply.

   _____
   _____
   _____

8. What will you do to work on yourself to the point where you become your life purpose?

   _____
   _____
   _____

❖ Exploring your purpose will help keep you focused. When you are prompted to make decisions, you may ask yourself the following questions: Is this aligned with my purpose? Is this going against my purpose?

NOTES:

Principle 3.
ALIGNMENT

How do you plan to get there?

This principle provides the opportunity for you to review, reflect, and *step outside the boundaries!* You must answer and be truthful with yourself. Have you identified what you truly desire, and are you prepared to move forward?

Now is the time to acknowledge that you are committed to achieving what you desire. What is important is to reflect on and review the first two principles. For example, the values you listed earlier may be a result of how you have been previously conditioned to respond. However, now that you have defined your vision, your values may not be aligned to support the course of your life direction.

For example, your vision may include acknowledging that you want to achieve a greater level of success, which was not listed in your top five values. At this point, you will have to go back to the first two principles and *reexamine* them to acknowledge and include the desire you have held close to your heart. To ensure alignment and live with integrity, *connect* and make the necessary changes as they apply to *balance, values, brand, vision, goals,* and *purpose*.

The last step is to *confirm* that all aspects support what you want to achieve in life.

Alignment focuses on reexamine, connect, and confirm.

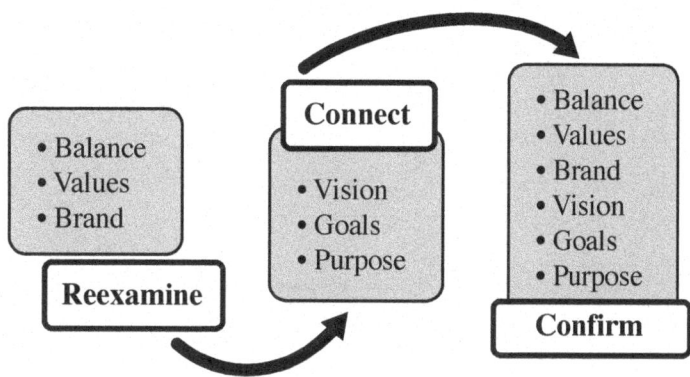

ALIGNMENT

Purpose:

Reexamine – Provides the opportunity to look at your life and confirm what you want to achieve.

Connect – Take another look at all areas: balance, values, brand, visions, goals, and purpose; make any necessary changes.

Confirm – Review all aspects that support what you want out of life.

Actions:

Reexamine – Determine if and where you are playing it safe or maintaining the status quo.

Connect – Make necessary changes to ensure all elements of the fundamental principles support the direction you want to go.

Confirm – Ensure all aspects of the first two fundamental principles are in sync.

Intended outcomes:

Reexamine – Know what you want in life and the approach to achieve it.

Connect – Commit to live according to your desires and be the fullest expression of self.

Confirm – Focus on a positive approach to your future.

ALIGNMENT
Reexamine, connect, and confirm:

Remember the old saying "If you do what you've always done, you'll get what you've always gotten"? Now is the time to make changes; to thy own self be true. This is about you!

1. Have you been playing it safe and maintaining the status quo? If so, what different approach will you take?

   _____
   _____
   _____

2. Look at what you want to achieve. Circle any areas that are out of sync.
   - Balance
   - Values
   - Brand
   - Vision
   - Goals
   - Purpose

3. If applicable, why are they out of sync? What are the consequences?

   _____
   _____
   _____

4. Now that you have defined your vision and goals, do you need to make any changes to your top five values to ensure alignment? If so, what changes do you need to make? List your top five values below.

   1. _____
   2. _____
   3. _____
   4. _____
   5. _____

5. What would it take for you to be, or continue to be, in alignment with your values, vision, goals, and purpose and tap into the essence of self? What change(s) do you need to make? What action(s) will you take?

   _____
   _____
   _____

ALIGNMENT
Reexamine, connect, and confirm:

6. What is the impact in the way you live and work?

   _____
   _____
   _____

7. What commitment(s) will you make? What is the time frame?

   _____
   _____
   _____

- ❖ Now that you are synced up, when you are prompted to make decisions, you may ask yourself the following questions: Is this decision aligned with my desires? Is this decision a detriment to my desires?

NOTES:

NOTES:

Principle 4.
AUTHENTICITY

Do you have the confidence to move forward?

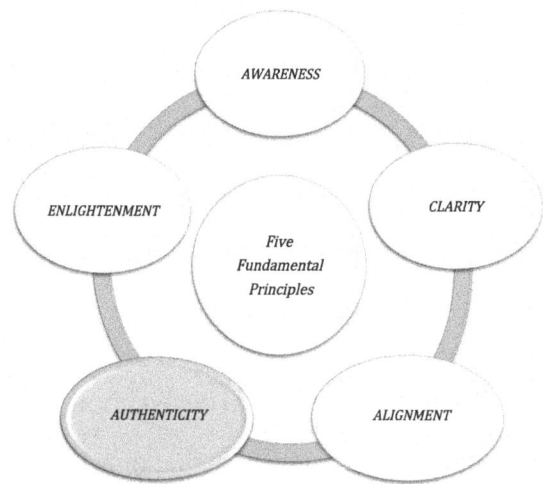

*T*his is the most significant principle. *To be honest and true to yourself is the key to living the life you desire.* You can complete all the work of the prior three principles, but if you don't make conscious choices and decisions that support what you want out of life, you will not achieve it.

In this principle, you will learn that there are obstacles in life that can prevent you from moving forward. These can be obstacles that you are not aware of unless you seek them out and understand what influence they have over you. You will assess what you need to do to show up and be your authentic self. This includes letting go of and surrendering to those things that hold you back and learning to embrace *you*.

You must focus on your mind-set, live your purpose, nurture a sense of belief, expect positive outcomes, and speak positive words about yourself. This will require the integrity for you to remain consistent with your actions, disciplined, obedient, and responsible. Take ownership for what you want.

Authenticity focuses on acknowledge, surrender, and embrace.

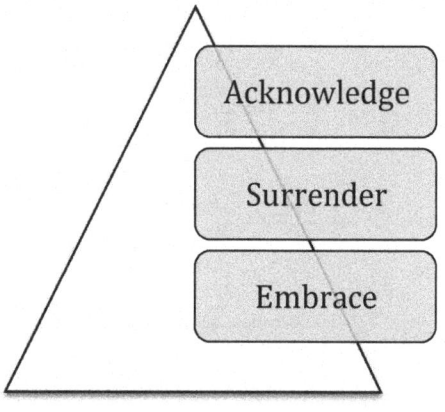

AUTHENTICITY

Purpose:

Acknowledge – Recognize and identify negative influences.

Surrender – Determine what may be holding you back.

Embrace – Provide the opportunity to focus on you.

Actions:

Acknowledge – Helps you deal with negative influences.

Surrender – Address issues that may be holding you back.

Embrace – Learn how to take actions and make decisions to support what you desire.

Intended outcomes:

Acknowledge – Supportive environment.

Surrender – Ability to move forward.

Embrace – Gain new insight and approach to living.

AUTHENTICITY
Acknowledge:

Now that you have a plan to accomplish what you want to achieve, recognize there are negative influences and surroundings that can prevent you from moving forward. These influences can be internal, external, or both.

Internal Influences

Let's begin with the negative voice inside your head saying that you don't have what it takes to achieve your desires. Your inner voice may also tell you that you are not good enough and fill your mind with negative thoughts. In coaching, this voice is referred to as the saboteur, and it is the master of trying to hold you back. The saboteur wants you to remain status quo and will do whatever it can to stop you from growing. Learn to recognize the voice and behavior of the saboteur. It has many disguises and can show up as anxiety, procrastination, or irritability. When you find yourself experiencing this behavior, know that it could be the saboteur and call it out: "Saboteur, you have no power over me." The more you recognize the saboteur and call it out, the weaker it becomes and the stronger you will become.

Another internal influence is how you feel about others and yourself. If you are harboring negative feelings or grudges toward others or yourself, acknowledge them, make amends if necessary, and forgive. This includes forgiving yourself for disappointments or decisions you have made in the past. Give yourself permission to forgive if necessary. Harboring negative feelings can hold you back and prevent you from being your authentic self. When you don't forgive, you give your power away. Don't allow your internal feelings to stop you from growing and being your best.

External Influences

External influencers can be in the form of either the people in your life or your surroundings. You may have friends, family, or peers who don't want you to make changes. They want you to stay right where you are, will not be supportive, and speak negatively about your potential. In those instances, you may not want to share your vision with them. Learning to live the life you desire is a conscious choice. Once you make that choice, protect your vision, surround yourself with support, love, and positive influences, and stay focused and encouraged. You may notice that as you change, you tend to spend less time with people who are negative and not supportive of you. You will more than likely find yourself spending time with people who are positive and have similar interests.

AUTHENTICITY
Acknowledge:

Surroundings

Be aware and know that negativity may lurk in your physical environment such as your job, your supervisor, your partner, or your living conditions. Although you may not be able to move or make any immediate changes, you can still focus on your vision and goals. Continue to meditate about your vision daily, read it out loud, and keep it visible. This activity will strengthen your faith and belief in you. Eventually, you will be able to begin to make changes, even if it means taking small actions or baby steps to allow for more time. Until then, don't allow your surroundings to define who you are and what you want. Although it may be difficult, stay focused and positive. Don't give up; keep your vision in your heart. Be mindful and deliberate and have faith.

AUTHENTICITY
Acknowledge:

1. Are you familiar with the saboteur? If so, what is the experience like? How will you handle it differently?

   _____
   _____
   _____

2. What negative feelings or grudges are you harboring toward others? Whom do you need to forgive? How will you go about it?

   _____
   _____
   _____

3. As you think of your life, are there areas where you need to forgive yourself? Be specific.

   _____
   _____
   _____

4. How will you manage external influences (friends, family, coworkers) that are prohibiting you from success?

   _____
   _____
   _____

5. What impact, if any, do your surroundings have on your ability to achieve what you desire? How will you address this barrier?

   _____
   _____
   _____

❖ **Being aware of negative influences can help you address them and make the necessary changes. These are questions you may ask yourself: Is this influence impacting me negatively or positively? How will I handle a negative influence?**

AUTHENTICITY
Surrender: To Self

Fear and Doubt

You can work through the first three principles, but if you allow fear and doubt to prevent you from moving forward, you will not achieve your vision. Fear is like a cancer. If ignored, it will grow, take over your life, and eventually stop you from living life to the fullest. Fear is the most talked-about reason why individuals don't pursue what they want out of life. In some cases, fear can be so deep seated that you don't recognize it and are unable to connect to and work through the emotions on your own. You may have to seek support from a coach or a therapist.

Fear can cause anxiety, negative thinking, worrying, and irrational behavior. It may be difficult, but you can start by acknowledging and naming the negative, unpleasant feeling and symptom associated with it. For example, if you have a fear of rejection, think about the feeling that is associated with it. Try to substitute a positive feeling for a negative one. This process will allow you to attach a different feeling to the negative reaction. Turn the negative feeling into a positive by looking at it from the perspective that it is not rejection, but this is not meant for you at this time. You can think of the rejection as a way of letting something better come your way or knowing that this is not the path for you to take.

Fear and doubt are emotions that we all experience. They are natural feelings, and learning how to recognize and deal with them is ongoing. You cannot simply learn to conquer the feelings and then expect them to go away for good. Life is a process of ongoing evolution, and emotions are part of who we are. As you grow and step outside your comfort zone, you may experience the fear of vulnerability or feeling exposed. Vulnerability is often viewed as a sign of weakness. However, the ability to connect with your emotions, confront your fears, and open up is just the opposite. It is a sign of courage and strength. To own the ability to expose your feelings is so powerful. Sharing feelings can be a humbling and rewarding experience. Once you open up, there is nothing to hide behind or hold you back. You get to own who you are. You will be free.

You can allow fear to prevent you from achieving your vision, or your desire to fulfill your vision can outweigh the fear. As you meditate daily, focus on your vision and living authentically as the person you want to be. Think about what emotions you need to tap into and then address them. Have faith and expect the best. Life is not easy, so planning to live on purpose will not be any less challenging. It will probably be more so; however, challenges can teach you what you need to succeed. If you have setbacks, look at them as learning opportunities. This journey is a process, and the more you acknowledge your fears and doubts and have faith, the stronger you will become. Take the time to acknowledge and absorb the lessons learned and use them to keep moving forward. *Success is achieved by failure.*

AUTHENTICITY
Surrender: To Self

Ego and Pride

Ego and pride can also get in the way of achieving what you desire. When you focus on the person within, think about what qualities or characteristics could prevent you from giving your best. If there is anything that gets in the way, learn to recognize it and make the necessary changes to move forward in a positive way. Be deliberate and mindful of living according to your values, brand, vision, goals, and purpose. How you show up to others and feel about yourself is so important. Think of it as a trade-off: what you put into the universe comes back to you. *Focus on living your best life so you can achieve the best.*

AUTHENTICITY
Surrender: To Self

1. How comfortable are you with recognizing and acknowledging your fears?

   _____
   _____
   _____

2. What impact, if any, is fear having in preventing you from moving forward to achieve what you desire? If so, how? Be specific. What are you afraid of?

   _____
   _____
   _____

3. What roles, if any, do ego and pride play? Be specific.

   _____
   _____
   _____

4. What would happen if these obstacles were removed?

   _____
   _____
   _____

5. What do you need to acknowledge about yourself that will strengthen and support you?

   _____
   _____
   _____

6. What one thing can you do, beginning now, to move forward? When will it happen?

   _____
   _____
   _____

   ❖ Fear is such a powerful emotion—awareness is the key to overcoming it. As you move forward and make decisions, you may ask yourself the following questions: Am I making this decision out of fear? Am I allowing fear to hold me back?

AUTHENTICITY
Embrace:

The last aspect of authenticity is *embracing you*. Acknowledge and give yourself credit for being *you* and what you have accomplished. Far too often, we beat up on ourselves and are our own worst critics. We can do more harm than anyone else can. Realize and accept that you are worthy and good and can have what you want in life. Know that you deserve to live a fulfilling life, so claim what is yours. Remember to speak positive words and thoughts about yourself. Be kind to *you*.

Make it a daily habit to acknowledge something you like about yourself. Recognize the goodness in you. Make a list. Write it out in positive statements and read it out loud daily. I would also suggest, if you don't already have one, buying a journal and writing in it daily. It is a great way to express your emotions. It can also build confidence. When you go back and read it, you can see how far you have come.

Finally, celebrate *you*. Make it a habit to do something for *you* weekly. It doesn't have to be anything big. It can be something as small as lighting a candle, sitting quietly, and acknowledging your strengths, gifts, and talents. Take the time to appreciate *you*.

It will take time, but if you stay focused and make deliberate choices, eventually you will get to the point where you are *all in*—no turning back. You will know you can achieve what you desire and have the insight, patience, and faith to stay the course. Stay anchored in who you are and what you value and stand for.

AUTHENTICITY
Embrace:

1. What do you appreciate most about your life and achievements?

   _____
   _____
   _____

2. What decisions and choices are you making daily that support your vision and goals?

   _____
   _____
   _____

3. What decisions and choices are you making daily that are contrary to your vision?

   _____
   _____
   _____

4. How do you begin to approach life differently? What will you do?

   _____
   _____
   _____

5. What do you see as your biggest challenge? How will you deal with it?

   _____
   _____
   _____

6. What are your beliefs about the concept of a higher power? How will you use your beliefs to sustain momentum and remain true to yourself?

   _____
   _____
   _____

❖ Now that you are prepared to make conscious choices to pursue what you desire, as you make decisions, you may ask yourself the following questions: What will it take for me to show up and be my authentic self? Will this decision prevent me from being my authentic self?

NOTES:

NOTES:

Principle 5.
ENLIGHTENMENT

How do you gain a new outlook?

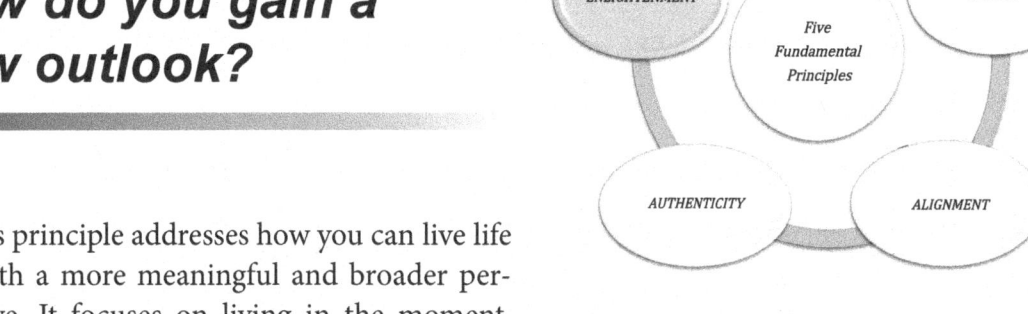

This principle addresses how you can live life with a more meaningful and broader perspective. It focuses on living in the moment, having peace of mind, and being grateful. Know that it takes time to create and live the life you desire, and doing so could involve a shift in belief and a change in behavior. However, you don't have to wait to experience enlightenment. It can begin now. Enlightenment is a state of mind and of being, looking at life and living it from a perspective of bliss.

You can experience enlightenment beginning with how you view life. Enlightenment is being able to recognize and embrace all aspects of your journey. It is about living life with a sense of purpose and joy, not taking anything for granted, and maintaining a positive attitude. As you begin to view life differently, you will be transformed and continue to evolve, experiencing enlightenment on deeper levels.

Enlightenment focuses on live in the moment, harmony, and gratitude.

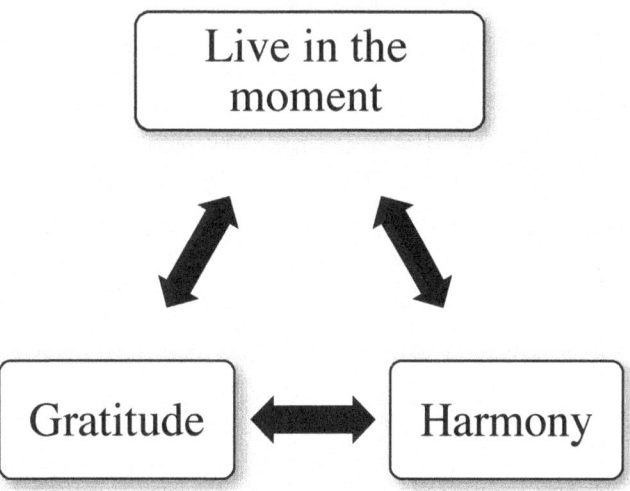

ENLIGHTENMENT
Purpose:
Live in the moment – Live life from a different perspective.

Harmony – Gain peace of mind.

Gratitude – Focus on a way of being.

Actions:
Live in the moment – Learn to be fully engaged in life.

Harmony – Experience fulfillment and connect to mind, body, and spirit.

Gratitude – Identify how to live being thankful.

Intended outcomes:
Live in the moment – Being present in all aspects of your life.

Harmony – Experiencing peace and freedom.

Gratitude – Appreciating life.

ENLIGHTENMENT
Live in the moment:

There is much to appreciate in life. Oftentimes, we are so busy focusing on tomorrow, our next thing to do, meetings, or something in the future that we fail to experience the present and live in the moment. All we have is the present. When we take time to be fully engaged, that engagement can lead to a very different life experience.

When you focus on living in the present, all of your focus and attention is on that moment. This focus allows you to see, feel, hear, and experience everything that is part of that moment, including your surroundings. This approach takes the focus off of only you and includes everything, both in you and surrounding you. You begin to feel and be connected to something much greater than yourself, creating new experiences on how you view and live your life.

Being present and fully engaged with your surroundings creates the awareness that you are part of the universe. Every aspect of life surrounds you: human beings, nature, and everything around us. When you are aware of and engage with the universe, the universe engages with you in return. This exchange can be amazing! At the very moment when you need reassurance, the wind touches your cheek in such a way that you know everything will work out for the best. Or you hear the sound of a bird, and it seems like it is singing just for you.

When you think about life in this way, even your interaction with others may elicit different experiences. You may find yourself having greater respect and appreciation for others' existence and recognize that we are all essentially the same. You may learn something from others simply by being present. There may be a message for you, the confirmation you have been seeking. Be present!

To engage and be present, spend time on the following:
- Fully connect with others.
- Practice listening.
- Notice your surroundings.
- Spend time outdoors; go for walks.
- Notice the smells, colors, and sound of the outdoors and the indoors.
- Notice and enjoy the air you breathe.
- Engage in the feeling that you are part of something bigger.

ENLIGHTENMENT
Live in the moment:

1. Is this way of thinking a new approach for you? If so, how is it different?

   _____
   _____
   _____

2. What impact, if any, will this perspective have on you?

   _____
   _____
   _____

ENLIGHTENMENT
Harmony:

This aspect of enlightenment addresses peace of mind. At this point, you have completed the actions and assessments identified in the previous principles. Now that you know what you want in life, begin to think about how it will feel once you achieve what you desire. Focus on the sense of fulfillment. Begin by identifying words that describe feelings of fulfillment: success, joy, accomplishment, independence, and security. During your daily meditation, allow yourself to connect with these feelings in your mind, body, and spirit. This connection will strengthen your beliefs and allow you to experience internal peace and freedom because you know you can and will achieve what you want from life.

Although you will become stronger in your beliefs, that doesn't mean that you will achieve what you desire immediately. However, you will know that you are on track and feel better about your life. The stronger you become, the less internal distraction and doubt show up. With less distraction comes greater peace of mind.

The following can help you focus on peace of mind:
- Meditate daily—visualize your dreams.
- Write out the details of how it feels to achieve fulfillment.
- Expect goodness in your life.
- Think and live as if you have already achieved your goals.
- Have faith.
- Write out positive affirmations and read them daily.
- Stay positive.
- Surround yourself with positive influences.

1. Is there anything preventing you from living in harmony? If so, what?

   _____
   _____
   _____

2. How, if possible, will this be a different experience for you? Do you have any concerns?

   _____
   _____
   _____

3. What changes, if any, will you make?

   _____
   _____
   _____

ENLIGHTENMENT
Gratitude:

The last aspect of enlightenment is gratitude. Gratitude is a state of being and a way of living. You have the choice to live with an appreciation for life and be grateful for all there is. This approach allows you to connect to the universe and be grateful for everything that exists. When you are grateful, you want to share that feeling with the world. You start each day excited, with joy, and expecting the best; you smile more, make eye contact, compliment others, and live with a sense of freedom.

Living with gratitude can have an enormous positive impact on others. Gratitude can be contagious. People will want what you have. It is that knowing that whatever is going on in your life, there is much to be grateful for because circumstances could always be worse. Even in your darkest hour, you remain grateful, knowing that eventually the sun will rise.

Take time during the day to acknowledge the goodness in your life. Allow it to become a part of who you are. To express gratitude, focus on the following:

- Begin each morning acknowledging what things you are grateful for—at least ten of them.
- Every morning, be excited for the opportunity to live another day.
- Respect and appreciate life; it is a gift. Cherish it.
- Know that the more grateful you are, the more you will have to be grateful for.
- Become a volunteer and help others.
- Appreciate who you are.
- Share freely and willingly.
- Be grateful for others and know that it is not always about you.

1. What would it take to start experiencing life with a sense of gratitude?

    _____
    _____
    _____

2. What changes, if any, do you need to make? When will you do it?

    _____
    _____
    _____

ENLIGHTENMENT
Gratitude:

3. What are you most grateful for? Why?

_____
_____
_____

❖ Now that you are prepared to live life with a broader perspective, throughout the day, you may ask yourself the following questions: Am I living in the present? Do I have peace of mind? Am I grateful?

NOTES:

Summary

Principle 1. AWARENESS—balance, values, brand

1. How do you view your current life situation? What changes do you need to make?

_____
_____
_____

Principle 2. CLARITY—vision, goals, purpose

2. Do you now have clarity on how you will live your life?

_____
_____
_____

Principle 3. ALIGNMENT—reexamine, connect, confirm

3. How will you stay synced up to support your future decisions?

_____
_____
_____

Principle 4. AUTHENTICITY—acknowledge, surrender, embrace

4. Explain how the three elements of authenticity have impacted how you feel about yourself and what you can achieve.

_____
_____
_____

Principle 5. ENLIGHTENMENT—live in the moment, harmony, gratitude

5. Are you enlightened to live your life differently? How?

_____
_____
_____

Show up your best. Give your best. Live your best!
~~ Be contagious ~~

SUMMARY

Witness the Most Powerful You is a self-development process that enables you to make the right decisions and choices to achieve your personal and professional goals. You may want to consider an accountability partner for support. You are responsible and accountable for what you want to achieve. How you use this process will help you grow and create the life you desire. Make decisions and choices that are aligned with what you want to achieve. Have faith, stay focused, and to thyself be true.

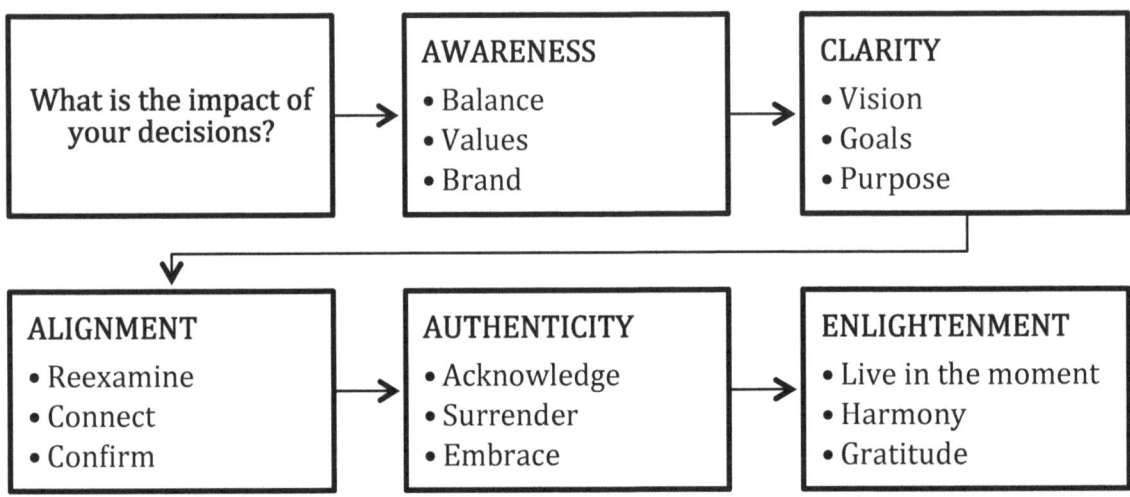

SUMMARY
Testimonials

"I learned that I need to accept who I am. It's me. Live life according to my values. I learned to let go of my fears and stop holding back." ~D.S.

"This has reopened a door that fear had closed for too long in my life!" ~V.L.

"I like the fact that I was prompted to think on a deeper level about writing or verbalizing my goals and my vision." ~E.C.

"The power of planning and reevaluation. I never acknowledge my talents or moments that I was most happy." ~K.J.

"This gave me permission to think about me and what I need to do for myself!" ~C.N.

NOTES:

Bibliography

Kimsey-House, Henry, Karen Kimsey-House, Phillip Sandahl, and Laura Whitworth. *Co-Active Coaching: Changing Business Transforming Lives.* Nicholas Brealey Publishing, 2011.

Peters, Tom. "The Brand Called YOU." *Fast Company Magazine.* August/September 1997.

Brown, Brene'. *The Gifts Of Imperfection.* Hazelden Publishing, 2010.

Tolle, Eckhart. *The Power of Now: A Guide to Spiritual Enlightenment.* Namaste Publishing Inc., 1997.

Dyer, Dr. Wayne W. *The Secrets to Manifesting Your Destiny.* Nightingale Conant.

Montoya, Peter, Tim Vandehey. *the brand called YOU.* Personal Branding Press, 2003.

About the Author

Eva M. Kennedy is the founder and principal of Eva M. Kennedy/1Evalution LLC. She is a business and life coach, speaker, and facilitator.

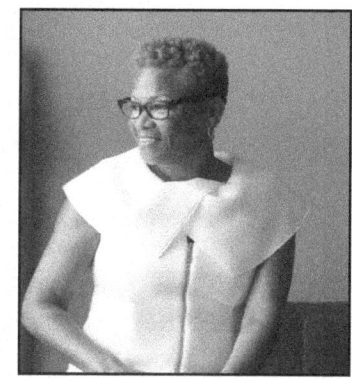

Eva is an accomplished professional with over twenty years of business-management and leadership experience. She achieved a key leadership role at Allstate Insurance Company as a director in the claims department. She was responsible for designing, developing, and implementing countrywide operations procedures with a $4 billion dollar impact on fifteen thousand employees. Eva is highly trained in career and leadership development, change management and transition roles, organizational strategy, and development.

After being diagnosed with breast cancer and having a reoccurrence within five years, she took early retirement and left the corporate world in 2006. Although cancer is a horrific disease, she would not trade anything for her journey.

During the past few years, Eva has been on a journey of self-discovery, which led her to coaching. She wanted to pursue her passion to help others, continue her own development, and find her purpose. While going through coaching training and having a personal coach, Eva was able to acknowledge and connect with her fears, which was the beginning of her transformation. This transformation allowed Eva to tap into the true essence of self and find her purpose in life: being a business and life coach and empowering others through awareness and clarity to embrace and live the lives they desire.

Eva is excited and passionate about helping others make meaningful life changes. She focuses on being her best for her clients and everyone around her. Eva is an active volunteer. She believes in giving back and enjoys working with others in any capacity to help them move forward.

Eva received her certified professional co-active certification (CPCC) from the Coaches Training Institute (CTI), an affiliate member of the Institute of Coaching Professional Association (ICPA). In addition, Eva received her associate certified coach (ACC) from the International Coach Federation (ICF), of which she is also an active member. She received her bachelor of science degree in business administration from Southern New Hampshire University.

You can contact Eva at her company, 1Evalution.com, or via e-mail at 1evalutioncc@gmail.com.